COMMON CORE CLINICS

Grade 5

Mathematics

Number, Operations and Algebraic Thinking

Common Core Clinics, Mathematics, Number, Operations and Algebraic Thinking, Grade 5
OT320 / 412NA

ISBN: 978-0-7836-8494-9

Author: Rebecca Motil
With special thanks to mathematics consultants:
Debra Harley, Director of Math/Science K–12, East Meadow School District
Allan Brimer, Math Specialist, New Visions School, Freeport School District
Cover Image: © gthompsonphotography/Veer

Triumph Learning® 136 Madison Avenue, 7th Floor, New York, NY 10016

© 2012 Triumph Learning, LLC
Options™ is an imprint of Triumph Learning®

ALL ABOUT YOUR BOOK

COMMON CORE CLINICS MATH will help you with key concepts.

A **Key Words** box introduces new math words. An **Example** shows you how to solve problems in the lesson.

Each lesson has **Guided Practice**. Hints called **THINK** and **REMEMBER** help you work through the problem.

There are two pages of **Independent Practice** with problems for you to solve on your own. You will also solve some **Word Problems**.

At the back of your book, there is a **Glossary** and **Math Tools** that will help you work out problems.

Module 1

Operations and Algebraic Thinking; Number and Operations in Base Ten

Key Words

expression
operation signs
parentheses

An **expression** is a combination of numbers and **operation signs** such as $+$, $-$, $\times$, and $\div$. **Parentheses** show which operation to do first. Examples of expressions are:

Expression in Words	Numerical Expression
the sum of 12 and 16	$12 + 16$
the difference of 9 and 4, then multiply by 8	$(9 - 4) \times 8$ or $8 \times (9 - 4)$
divide 350 by 3, then add 1	$(350 \div 3) + 1$ or $1 + (350 \div 3)$

Example

Lyle bought a ticket to a soccer game for $16. He paid with a $20 bill.

Write an expression to show how much change Lyle received.

Write the expression using words.

$20 minus the cost of the ticket
$20 minus $16

Write the expression using numbers.

$20 - 16$

Lyle's change can be shown by the expression $20 - 16$.

LIST

Words such as *sum* and *more* tell you to add.

List two words that tell you to subtract.

List two words that tell you to multiply.

List two words that tell you to divide.

Guided Practice

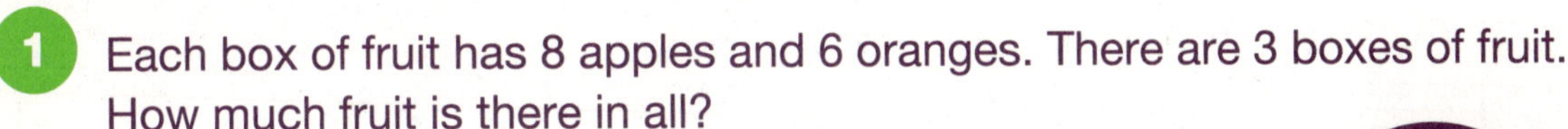

1 Each box of fruit has 8 apples and 6 oranges. There are 3 boxes of fruit. How much fruit is there in all?

Write an expression to show the total amount of fruit.

THINK

Add the apples and oranges to get the amount of fruit in each box.

Step 1 Write the expression in words.

______ times the sum of ______ and ______

Step 2 Write an expression using numbers and operation signs.

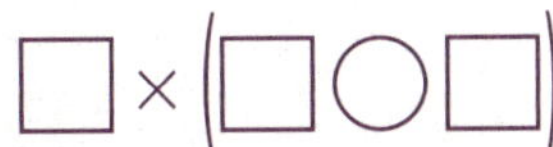

REMEMBER

Parentheses show which operation to do first.

The expression is _____________.

2 At the Shack, 31 burgers sold in the first hour and 15 burgers sold in each of the next 5 hours. How many burgers were sold in all?

Write an expression to show the total number of burgers sold.

REMEMBER

An expression does not have an equal sign.

Step 1 Write the expression in words.

______ plus the product of ______ and ______

Step 2 Write an expression using numbers and operation signs.

$\square + (\square \bigcirc \square)$

The expression is _____________.

Independent Practice

1. Is $3 \times (4 + 2)$ an expression? Explain why or why not.

____

____

2. When writing an expression, when should you use parentheses?

____

____

Ask Yourself

Which operation or operations should I use?

Do I need to include parentheses?

Write an expression.

3. the difference of 492 and 389 _______________________

4. the product of 25 and 10 _______________________

5. 14 plus the product of 12 and 15 _______________________

6. the quotient of 45 and 9, plus 6 _______________________

7. add 6 and 12, then divide by 2 _______________________

8. Dinner costs $24. You give the cashier $30. Write an expression to show the change you will receive.

____

Write an expression.

9. subtract 36 from 100, then multiply by 8 _______________________

10. the sum of 382 and 420, divided by 2 _______________________

11. add 4 and 7, then multiply by 16 _______________________

12. divide the product of 50 and 3 by 5, then add 2 _______________________

13. 40 cars divided equally among 5 rows _______________________

14. 3 trays of ice cubes with 12 cubes per tray, plus 4 cubes gone

____

15. 20 seats with 2 students per seat and 1 student extra _______________________

Solve each problem.

16. Tickets to the school play cost $6 per person. The school
    made $3,168 selling tickets. Write an expression to show
    how many tickets were sold.

    ____

17. On a backpacking trip, Cara hiked 20 miles in two days.
    The first day she hiked 12 miles. Write an expression to
    show how many miles Cara hiked the second day.

    ____

Key Words

order of operations

Some expressions have more than one operation. To find the value of these expressions, use the **order of operations**.

- First, do any operations in parentheses.
- Next, multiply and divide from left to right.
- Then, add and subtract from left to right.

Example

Evaluate the expression.

$18 - 4 \times 3$

There are no parentheses, so start by multiplying from left to right.

$18 - 4 \times 3$

$\downarrow$

$18 - \quad 12$

Then subtract.

$18 - 12$

$\downarrow$

6

The value of the expression is 6.

APPLY

Which is greater, $(8 + 4) \times 3$ or $8 + 4 \times 3$? Explain your reasoning.

Guided Practice

Evaluate the expression.

$(4 + 11) \div 3 + 7$

Step 1 Use the order of operations.
Start by finding the sum in parentheses.

$(4 + 11) \div 3 + 7$

↓

________ $\div 3 + 7$

Step 2 Next, multiply and divide from left to right.

________ $\div 3 + 7$

↓

________ $+ 7$

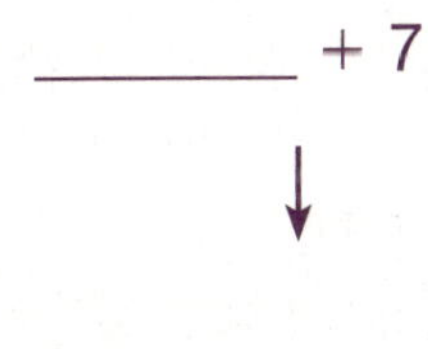

Step 3 Then, add and subtract from left to right.

________ $+ 7$

↓

____

The value of the expression is ________.

Independent Practice

1. How do you use the order of operations to evaluate an expression?

____

____

2. A calculator displays 38 as the value of $8 + 3 \times 10$. Does the calculator follow the order of operations? Explain.

____

____

Ask Yourself

What do I do when I see parentheses in an expression?

Which operation should I perform first?

Look at each expression. If the order of operations is listed in the correct order, write *correct*. If not, write the correct order of operations.

3. $(10 + 8) \times 6$ multiply, add   __________

4. $3 \times (11 - 5)$ subtract, multiply   __________

5. $22 + 8 \div 10$ add, divide   __________

6. $39 - 14 + 12$ subtract, add   __________

7. For a field trip, museum admission is $12 and lunch for each person is $6. Twenty-five students will go on the field trip. Write an expression to show the total cost of the trip.

____

Evaluate the expression. What is the total cost of the trip?

____

Find the value of each expression.

8. $6 \times 9 + 2$

____

9. $128 \div (10 - 6)$

____

10. $375 - 75 \times 2$

____

11. $(16 + 8) \div 4 - 5$

____

Evaluate each expression. Then write <, >, or =.

12. $12 + 6 \bigcirc 12 + 7$

____

13. $4 \times (372 + 8) \bigcirc 372 + 8$

____

14. $10 \times (1,025 - 25) \bigcirc (1,025 - 25) \times 10$

____

15. $40 \times 8 \div 2 \bigcirc 20 \times 8 \div 2$

____

Solve each problem.

16. There are 7 packs of pencils. Each pack has 8 pencils. Ms. Ward gives 4 pencils from one pack to students. Write an expression to show how many pencils are in the packs now. Then evaluate it.

____

17. Which is greater, $18 + 13$ or $5 \times (18 + 13)$? Explain your reasoning.

____

18. Use the numbers 1, 2, 3, and 4 exactly once to write an expression with a value of 9.

____

3 Patterns

A **number sequence** is a list of numbers such as: 0, 3, 6, 9, 12. The numbers, or **terms**, in a sequence often follow a pattern. In the number sequence above, the pattern is that each term is 3 greater than the number before it.

You can use a rule to describe a **number pattern**. The **rule** for a pattern is a relationship between the terms in that pattern. The rule for the pattern above is: add 3.

To find the next term in the pattern, add 3 to the number before it.

$$\text{So, } 0 + 3 = 3$$
$$3 + 3 = 6$$
$$6 + 3 = 9$$
$$9 + 3 = 12$$
$$12 + 3 = 15 \quad \text{The next term in the pattern is 15.}$$

Example

Find the rule for the number pattern: 30, 25, 20, 15. Then find the next term in the pattern.

First, find the rule.

The difference between each number is 5.

$$30 - 5 = 25$$
$$25 - 5 = 20$$
$$20 - 5 = 15$$

The rule is: subtract 5.

Next, use the rule to find the next term in the pattern.

Subtract 5 from 15.

$$15 - 5 = 10$$

The next term in the pattern is 10.

APPLY

The rule for a number pattern is multiply by 2. The starting number is 5. What are the first four numbers in the pattern?

Guided Practice

1 Find the rule for this number pattern: 96, 48, 24, 12.

    Step 1 Look for a relationship between the terms in the pattern.

    Are the numbers increasing or decreasing? ______________

    Which operations should you consider as you look for the rule?

    _____________________ and _____________________

    Step 2 Find the rule.

    Each number is half the number before it.

    $96 \div 2 = 48$

    $48 \div \underline{\quad} = 24$

    $24 \div \underline{\quad} = 12$

The rule is: divide by ______.

2 Find the rule for this number pattern: 4, 8, 16, 32.
Then find the next term in the sequence.

    Step 1 Find the rule.

    Each number is ______ times the number before it.

    $4 \times \underline{\quad} = 8$

    $8 \times \underline{\quad} = 16$

    $16 \times \underline{\quad} = 32$

The rule is: multiply by ______.

    Step 2 Find the next term in the pattern.

    Use the rule to find the next number.

    $32 \bigcirc \underline{\quad} = \underline{\quad}$

The next term in the pattern is ______.

REMEMBER

Look for a pattern to help you find the rule. Test it on all the numbers in the pattern.

THINK

To find the next number, should I add, subtract, multiply, or divide? By how much?

Independent Practice

1. Each number in a pattern is less than the number before it. Which two operations should you use as you look for a rule? Explain.

____

____

2. Why is it important to test a rule on all the numbers in a pattern?

____

____

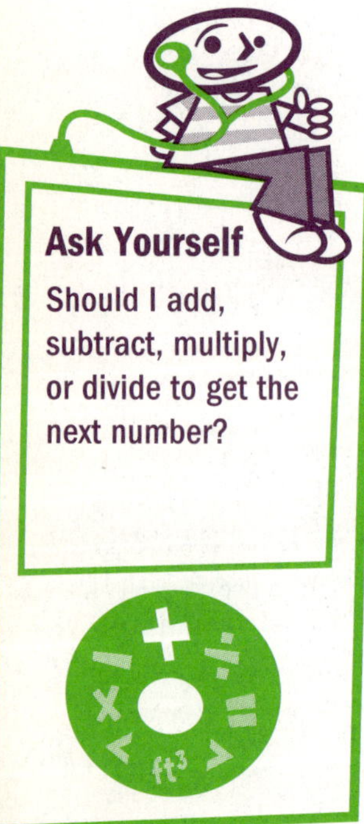

Ask Yourself

Should I add, subtract, multiply, or divide to get the next number?

Find a rule for the number pattern. Use the rule to write the next term in the sequence.

3. 6, 12, 18, 24, _______   Rule: _______________________

4. 2, 5, 8, 11, _______   Rule: _______________________

5. 63, 54, 45, 36, _______   Rule: _______________________

6. 4, 12, 36, 108, _______   Rule: _______________________

7. Lee is practicing for the basketball team. On Day 1 he makes 5 baskets, on Day 2 he makes 10 baskets, and so on. The table shows how many baskets Lee makes each day.

Day	1	2	3	4	5	6	7
Number of Baskets	5	10	15	20	25	30	?

If the pattern continues, how many baskets do you predict Lee will make on Day 7?

____

Find a rule for the number pattern. Use the rule to write the next term in the sequence.

8. 80, 40, 20, 10, _______   Rule: _____________________

9. 0, 10, 20, 30, _______   Rule: _____________________

10. 1, 5, 25, 125, _______   Rule: _____________________

11. 20, 26, 32, 38, _______   Rule: _____________________

12. 75, 65, 55, 45, _______   Rule: _____________________

13. 50, 43, 36, 29, _______   Rule: _____________________

14. 1, 22, 43, 64, _______   Rule: _____________________

Solve each problem.

15. Each week, Nyla increases the number of miles she walks. The first week she walks 3 miles, the next week 5 miles, and so on.

Complete the table to show how many miles Nyla walked in the sixth week.

Week	1	2	3	4	5	6
Miles Walked	3	5	7	9	11	

What is the rule for the miles Nyla walks each week?

____

16. Write a number pattern using the rule: subtract 3.

____

Key Words

coordinate plane
ordered pair
x-coordinate
y-coordinate

You can show the relationship between patterns on a **coordinate plane**. You can graph the values as **ordered pairs**. An ordered pair (x, y) is a pair of numbers used to locate a point on a coordinate grid.

The first number of the ordered pair is the **x-coordinate**. It tells distance from zero along the horizontal number line. The second number of the ordered pair is the **y-coordinate**. It tells distance from zero along the vertical number line.

Example

Find corresponding terms in the two patterns below. Write and graph the first three ordered pairs. How are the terms in the two patterns related?

Pattern 1: 0, 3, 6, 9, 12

Pattern 2: 0, 6, 12, 18, 24

In the number patterns, the first number in each pattern forms the first ordered pair: (0, 0). The second number in each pattern forms the second ordered pair: (3, 6). The third number in each pattern forms the third ordered pair: (6, 12).

Graph (0, 0). Place a point at 0 on the graph.

Graph (3, 6). Start at 0. Move 3 spaces to the right on the grid. Then move 6 spaces up on the grid.

Graph (6, 12). Start at 0. Move 6 spaces to the right on the grid. Then move 12 spaces up on the grid.

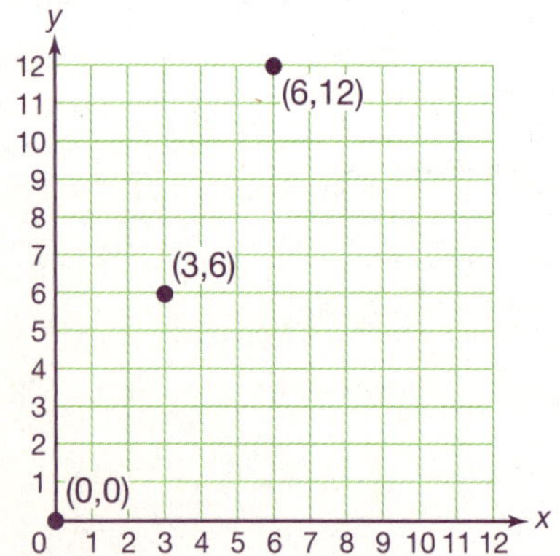

EXPLAIN

How would you graph the ordered pair (2, 4) on a coordinate grid?

The terms in Pattern 2 (the *y*-coordinates) are two times the value of the corresponding terms in Pattern 1 (the *x*-coordinates).

Guided Practice

Use the rule given below for each number pattern. Complete each pattern. Then graph the ordered pairs on the coordinate grid. How are the terms in the two patterns related?

Step 1 Use the rule to complete the number pattern to find the *x*-coordinates.

Add 1 to find the next number in the pattern. 0, 1, 2, _______

Step 2 Use the rule to complete the number pattern to find the *y*-coordinates.

Add 3 to find the next number in the pattern. 0, 3, 6, _______

Step 3 Write ordered pairs (*x*, *y*) using the corresponding terms from each pattern.

(0, _______)   (1, _______) (2, _______) (_______, _______)

The ordered pairs are _________, _________, _________, _________.

Step 4 Graph the ordered pairs on a coordinate grid.

Start at 0. Move right as many spaces as the first number in the ordered pair tells you.

Then move up as many spaces as the second number tells you.

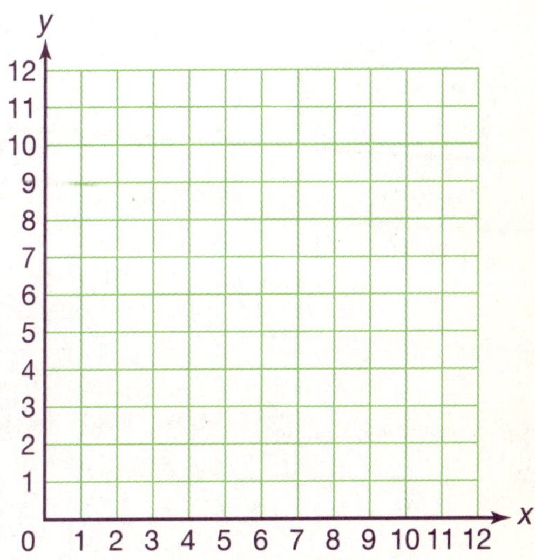

Step 5 Compare the terms to see how they are related.

$$y = x \times 3$$

$$3 = 1 \times 3$$

$$6 = 2 \times 3$$

$$9 = \underline{\quad} \times \underline{\quad}$$

The value of the *y*-coordinate is _______ times the value of the *x*-coordinate.

Independent Practice

1. How can you use an ordered pair (x, y) to locate a point on a coordinate grid?

____

____

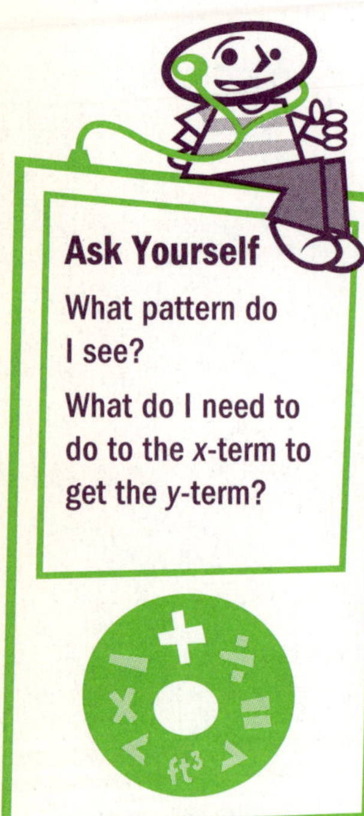

For questions 2–5, complete each pattern. Then graph the ordered pairs on the coordinate grid. How are the terms in the two patterns related?

2. Complete each pattern.

   Rule: Add 2. x-coordinates: 0, 2, _______, _______, _______

   Rule: Add 4. y-coordinates: 0, 4, _______, _______, _______

3. Write the ordered pairs. (0, 0), _______, _______, _______, _______

4. Graph the ordered pairs on the coordinate grid.

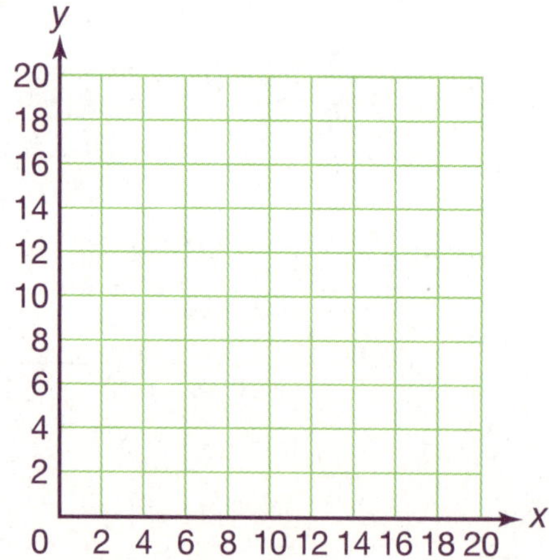

5. How are the corresponding terms (x, y) of the patterns related?

   ____

For questions 6 and 7, complete each pattern. Then write the ordered pairs.

6. Complete each pattern.

Rule: Add 5. 0, _______, _______, _______, _______

Rule: Add 10. 0, _______, _______, _______, _______

7. Write the ordered pairs. _______, _______, _______, _______, _______

Solve each problem.

Each week, a weightlifter increases the weights he lifts. The first week he lifts 10 pounds, the second week 20 pounds, the third week 30 pounds, and so on.

8. Complete the table to show the amount the weightlifter lifts each week.

Week (x-coordinate)	1	2	3	4	5
Amount Lifted (y-coordinate)	10				

9. Graph the ordered pairs (x, y) on the coordinate grid.

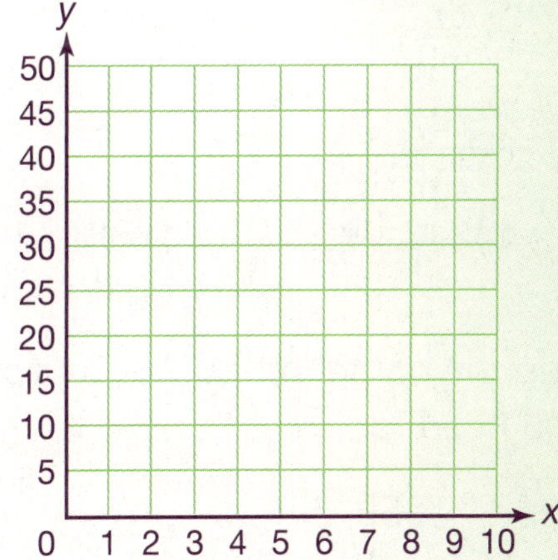

10. How are the corresponding terms (x, y) of the patterns related?

____

5 Multiply Whole Numbers

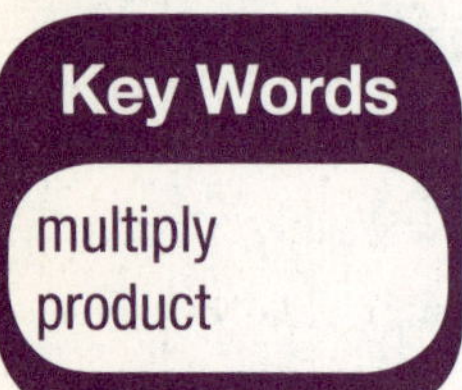

Key Words

multiply
product

When you **multiply** two numbers, the answer is called the **product**. To multiply larger numbers, follow the steps below. Estimate to check your work.

Example

Find the product of 356 and 42.

Line up the digits with the same place values.

```
  356
×  42
```

Multiply by the 2 in the ones place.

```
    1 1
  356
×  42
  712
```

2×6 ones $= 12$ ones. Regroup.
2×5 tens $= 10$ tens. Add the regrouped ten and regroup again.
2×3 hundreds $= 6$ hundreds. Add the regrouped hundred.

Multiply by the 4 in the tens place.
Regroup the tens and hundreds.

```
    2 2
  356
×  42
  712
14240
```

← Write a 0 in the ones place as a placeholder.

Add the partial products. Regroup if you need to.

```
     356
×     42
     712     ← 2 × 356
+ 14 240     ← 40 × 356
  14,952     ← 42 × 356
```

$42 \times 356 = 14,952$

Guided Practice

Find the product.

35 × 206

Step 1   Rewrite the problem vertically.

206
× 35

Step 2   Multiply by 5. Regroup if needed.

3
206
× 35
1030

Step 3   Multiply by 3 tens. Write a 0 in the ones place before multiplying. Regroup if needed.

$$
\begin{array}{r}
\square\ \ \ \ \ \\
2\ 0\ 6 \\
\times\quad 3\ 5 \\
\hline
1\ 0\ 3\ 0 \\
\square\ \square\ \square\ 0 \\
\hline
\end{array}
$$

Step 4   Add the partial products.

$$
\begin{array}{r}
2\ 0\ 6 \\
\times\quad 3\ 5 \\
\hline
1\ 0\ 3\ 0 \\
+\ \square\ \square\ \square\ 0 \\
\hline
\square,\square\ \square\ \square \\
\end{array}
$$

35 × 206 = __________

REMEMBER

Line up the digits with the same place values.

THINK

5 × 6 ones = 30 ones
Regroup 30 as 3 tens.

5 × 0 tens = 0 tens
Add the regrouped tens.

5 × 2 hundreds = 10 hundreds
Regroup 10 hundreds as 1 thousand.

Independent Practice

1. How do you multiply a 2-digit number by a 2-digit number?

____

____

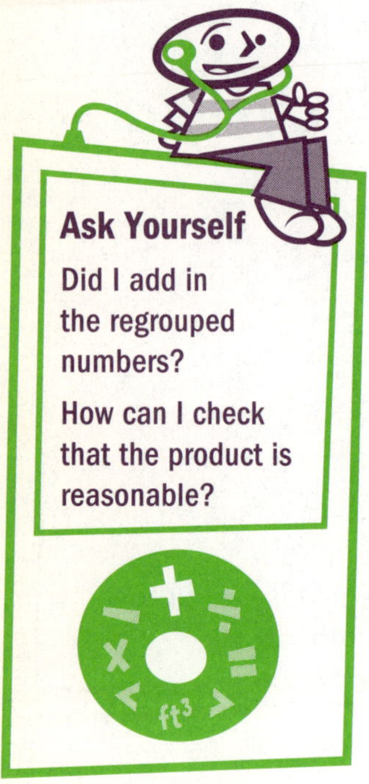

Ask Yourself

Did I add in the regrouped numbers?

How can I check that the product is reasonable?

For questions 2 through 7, line up the digits with the same place values and then multiply.

2. 54×22

3. 38×49

4. 780×14

5. 598×31

6. Tickets to the Science Center cost \$12 each. How much will tickets cost for 27 students?

____

7. A machine makes 264 magnets per minute. How many magnets can the machine make in 15 minutes?

____

Find each product.

8. 59 × 24

9. 76 × 50

10. 321 × 18

11. 186 × 40

12. 504 × 37

13. 725 × 27

14. 6,134 × 52

15. 5,078 × 77

16. 25 × 40

17. 120 × 15

18. 712 × 33

19. 8,236 × 61

Solve each problem.

20. The average dishwasher uses 15 gallons of water per load. Ms. Portman used her dishwasher 29 times last month. How many gallons of water did she use?

____

21. Membership at a gym costs $348 per year. In January, 87 people joined the gym. How much did the gym collect in membership fees?

____

6 Divide Whole Numbers

Key Words

divide
dividend
divisor
quotient
remainder

When you **divide** two numbers, the answer is the **quotient**. The number you are dividing by is the **divisor**. The number being divided is the **dividend**. The number that is left over after division is complete is the **remainder**.

$$\text{quotient} \rightarrow 64 \ \ R1 \leftarrow \text{remainder}$$
$$\text{divisor} \rightarrow 5\overline{)321}$$
$$\uparrow$$
$$\textbf{dividend}$$

Example

Find the quotient of 167 and 3.

Write $3\overline{)167}$.

Estimate to place the first digit in the quotient.

$$\text{Think: } 3\overline{)150} \ \ \text{or} \ \ 3\overline{)180}$$

with estimates 50 and 60.

Place the first digit of the quotient in the tens place.

Divide 16 tens.

$$
\begin{array}{r}
5 \\
3\overline{)167} \\
-15 \\
\hline
1
\end{array}
$$

Divide: 16 tens ÷ 3
Multiply: $5 \times 3 = 15$
Subtract: $16 - 15 = 1$
Compare: $1 < 3$
Bring down the 7 ones.

Divide 17 ones.

$$
\begin{array}{r}
55 \ R2 \\
3\overline{)167} \\
-15 \\
\hline
17 \\
-15 \\
\hline
2
\end{array}
$$

Divide: 17 ones ÷ 3
Multiply: $5 \times 3 = 15$
Subtract: $17 - 15 = 2$
Compare: $2 < 3$
The remainder is 2.

$167 \div 3 = 55 \ R2$

ANALYZE

How do you know when a division is complete?

Guided Practice

Find the quotient.

487 ÷ 23

Step 1   Set up the division problem.

$$23\overline{)487}$$

Step 2   Estimate to place the first digit in the quotient.

$23\overline{)487}$ ← Place the first digit in the quotient

in the _______ place.

Step 3   Divide 48 tens.

$$\square$$
$$23\overline{)4\ 8\ 7}$$
$$-\ 4\ 6$$
$$\overline{2}$$

← _______ × 23 = 46

← 48 − 46 = _______

Step 4   Bring down the 7 ones.
Divide 27 ones.

$$\square\ \square\,R\,\square$$
$$23\overline{)4\ 8\ 7}$$
$$-\ 4\ 6$$
$$\overline{2\ 7}$$
$$-2\ 3$$
$$\overline{\square}$$

← 1 × 23 = _______

← 27 − 23 = _______

487 ÷ 23 = _______

REMEMBER

Keep dividing until
the remainder
is less than the
divisor.

Independent Practice

1. Explain how to find the first digit in the quotient of 529 ÷ 49.

____

____

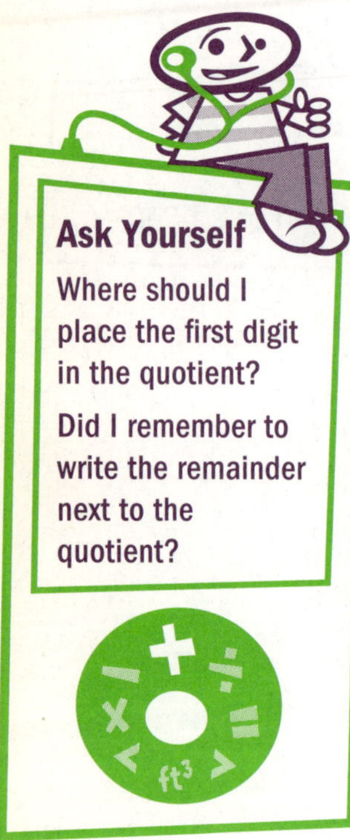

Find the quotient.

2. $4\overline{)216}$

3. $15\overline{)375}$

4. $7\overline{)682}$

5. $31\overline{)324}$

6. There are 450 seats in a theater. Each section has 50 seats. How many sections does the theater have?

____

7. Each egg carton holds 12 eggs. There are 280 eggs to be put in cartons. How many egg cartons can you fill completely? How many eggs will be left over?

____

Divide.

8. $2\overline{)128}$ **9.** $3\overline{)135}$ **10.** $10\overline{)602}$ **11.** $11\overline{)259}$

12. $25\overline{)475}$ **13.** $37\overline{)641}$ **14.** $52\overline{)585}$ **15.** $41\overline{)784}$

16. $19\overline{)4,484}$ **17.** $72\overline{)9,236}$ **18.** $43\overline{)1,247}$ **19.** $68\overline{)5,534}$

Solve each problem.

20. There are 270 children at soccer camp. The director divides them into 18 groups. How many children are in each group?

____

21. The band director wants the band to march in rows of 12. There are 165 band members. How many rows of 12 can they form? How many members will not be in a row of 12?

____

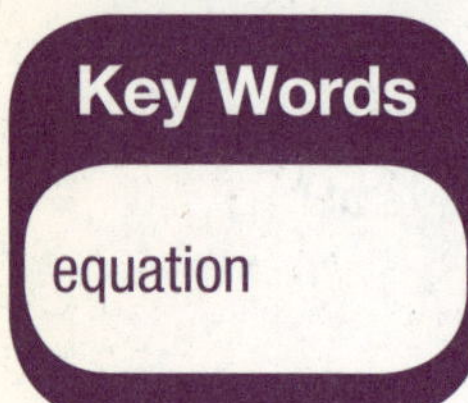

Key Words

equation

Recall that multiplication and division are related. For example:

$$4 \times 6 = 24 \qquad 24 \div 6 = 4$$

You can check a division problem by multiplying the quotient by the divisor and adding the remainder to the product. You can show this with an equation. An **equation** is a statement that two expressions are equal.

Example

Divide: $846 \div 24$. Write the result as an equation.

Divide.

```
        35 R6
   24)846
     − 72
      126
    − 120
        6
```

To check the answer, multiply the quotient by the divisor. Then add the remainder.

```
    35   ← quotient
  × 24   ← divisor
   140
 + 700
   840
 +   6   ← remainder
   846   ← This equals the dividend.
```

Write an equation.

$$\text{dividend} = \text{quotient} \times \text{divisor} + \text{remainder}$$
$$846 = 35 \times 24 + 6$$

The equation for the division is $846 = 35 \times 24 + 6$.

APPLY

After dividing, you found that $366 \div 4 = 91$ R2. How can you check your answer?

Guided Practice

Find the quotient. Write the result as an equation.

$2{,}174 \div 39$

Step 1 Divide.

$$\square\ \square\ R\ \square\ \square$$

$$39\overline{)2{,}174}$$
$$-\ 1\ 9\ 5$$
$$2\ 2\ 4$$
$$-\ 1\ 9\ 5$$
$$\square\ \square$$

Step 2 Check your answer.

$\square\ \square$ ← quotient
$\times\ \square\ \square$ ← divisor
$\square\ \square\ \square$
$+\ \square\ \square\ \square\ \square$
$\square{,}\square\ \square\ \square$
$+\ \square\ \square$ ← remainder
$\square{,}\square\ \square\ \square$ ← dividend

Step 3 Write an equation.

dividend = quotient × divisor + remainder

______ = ______ × ______ + ______

The equation for the division is ______________________________.

Independent Practice

1. How do you write a quotient as an equation when there is no remainder?

____

____

Ask Yourself

Did I remember to add the remainder to the product of the quotient and the divisor?

Does the left side of the equation equal the right side?

Divide. Then write the quotient as an equation.

2. $7\overline{)610}$

3. $4\overline{)312}$

$610 = $ _______________

$312 = $ _______________

4. $25\overline{)178}$

5. $13\overline{)489}$

$178 = $ _______________

$489 = $ _______________

6. Luna has 144 photos. Each page of her photo album holds 6 photos.

a. How many pages does Luna need to hold all her photos?

____

b. Write the quotient as an equation.

____

Divide. Then write the quotient as an equation.

7. $22\overline{)137}$

____

8. $60\overline{)374}$

____

9. $14\overline{)890}$

____

10. $35\overline{)956}$

____

11. $34\overline{)1,326}$

____

12. $75\overline{)3,162}$

____

Solve each problem.

Each picture frame uses 34 in. of wood. Ajeet has 410 in. of wood.

13. How many picture frames can Ajeet make? How many inches of wood will he have left over?

____

14. Write the quotient as an equation.

____

8 Read and Write Decimals

A **decimal** names wholes and parts of a whole. The **decimal point (.)** separates the ones from the tenths.

One tenth is shaded.

One hundredth is shaded.

One thousandth is shaded.

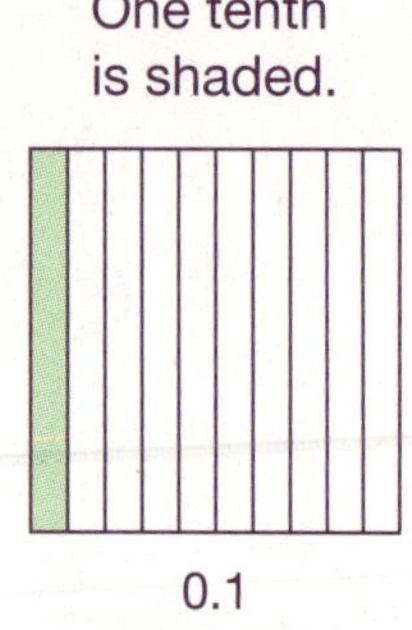

0.1
one tenth

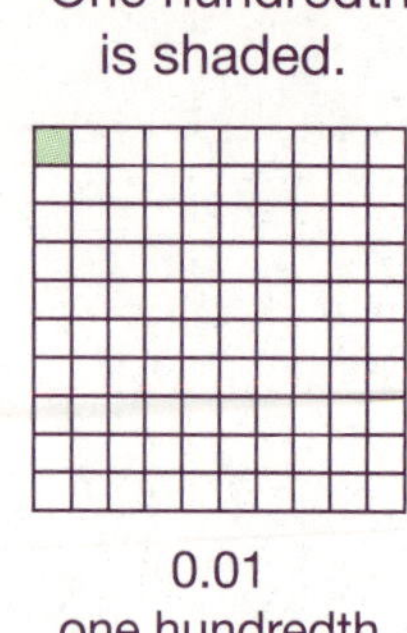

0.01
one hundredth

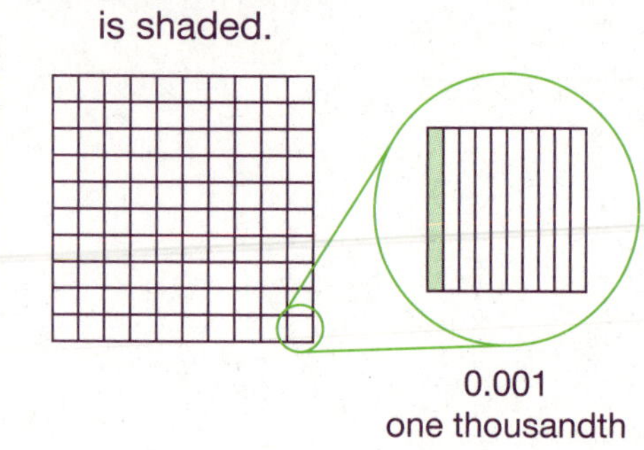

0.001
one thousandth

You can use a place-value chart to find the value of each digit in a decimal.

Example

Write the decimal 285.13 as a base-ten numeral and in expanded form. Then write its number name.

Find the value shown by each digit in the number 285.13. Notice that as you move from right to left on a place-value chart, the value of each place is 10 times greater than the value of the place to its right.

	Hundreds	Tens	Ones	.	Tenths	Hundredths
Base-Ten Numeral	2	8	5	.	1	3
Expanded Form	2×100	8×10	5×1	.	1×0.1	3×0.01

When you read and write a decimal, use the word "and" to separate the whole-number part from the decimal part.

base-ten numeral: 285.13

expanded form: $2 \times 100 + 8 \times 10 + 5 \times 1 + 1 \times 0.1 + 3 \times 0.01$

number name: two hundred eight-five and thirteen hundredths

INTERPRET

Write a rule for the pattern you see as you move from right to left in a place-value chart.

Guided Practice

Write the decimal 168.209 as a base-ten numeral and in expanded form.
Then write its number name.

Step 1 Complete the place-value chart.

	Hundreds	Tens	Ones	.	Tenths	Hundredths	Thousandths
Base-Ten Numeral	1		8	.			9
Expanded Form	____ × 100	____ × 10	____ × 1	.	____ × 0.1	____ × 0.01	____ × 0.001

Step 2 Write the decimal as a base-ten numeral. ________

Step 3 Write the decimal in expanded form.

________ × 100 + ________ × 10

+ ________ × 1 + ________ × 0.1

+ ________ × 0.001

Step 4 Write the decimal's number name.

THINK

There are 0 hundredths, so you do not have to include the hundredths place when you write the decimal in expanded form.

____________________________ and

____

The expanded form of 168.209 is ____________________________.

The number name of 168.209 is ____________________________.

Independent Practice

1. When writing a decimal's number name, how do you know where to write "and"?

____

____

2. Explain how the decimal 15.2 is different from the decimal 1.52.

____

____

Ask Yourself

What is the least place value in the decimal?

How should I show the decimal point when I write a decimal's number name?

3. Complete the place-value chart for 1.826.
Write the decimal as a base-ten numeral and in expanded form. Then write its number name.

	Ones	.	Tenths	Hundredths	Thousandths
Base-Ten Numeral					
Expanded Form	____ × 1	.	____ × 0.1	____ × 0.01	____ × 0.001

base-ten numeral: ____________________________

expanded form: ____________________________

number name: ____________________________

4. The normal human body temperature tends to be around 98.6 degrees Fahrenheit.

Write the temperature in expanded form.

____

Write the temperature as a number name.

____

Complete the place-value chart for the decimal. Write the decimal as a base-ten numeral and in expanded form. Then write its number name.

5. 50.954

	Tens	Ones	.	Tenths	Hundredths	Thousandths
Base-Ten Numeral			.			
Expanded Form			.			

base-ten numeral: _______________________

number name: _______________________________________

expanded form: _______________________________________

Write as a base-ten numeral.

6. five thousandths

____

7. one and forty-sixth hundredths

____

8. fifteen and eighty hundredths

____

9. seven hundred eighty-three and twenty-five thousandths

____

Solve each problem.

For a science experiment, Muhammad finds that the average length of a Coulter pine seed is 0.312 inch.

10. Write the length in expanded form. _______________________________

11. Write the length as a number name. _______________________________

9 Compare Decimals

You can use a number line or a place-value chart to compare decimals.

Example 1

Use a number line to compare.

2.65 ◯ 2.30

2.65 is to the right of 2.30, so it is greater.

2.65 is greater than 2.30

2.65 > 2.30

Example 2

Use a place-value chart to compare.

1.505 ◯ 1.542

Write the decimals in the place-value chart.
Then compare the decimals, beginning with the greatest place value.
Look for the greatest place where the digits are different.

Ones	.	Tenths	Hundredths	Thousandths
1	.	5	0	5
1	.	5	4	2

The digits in the hundredths place
are different.

Compare the digits.

0 < 4

So, 1.505 is less than 1.542.

1.505 < 1.542

Guided Practice

1   Use a number line to compare.

6.13 ◯ 6.294

Step 1   Plot each point on the number line.

Step 2   Compare.

6.13 is to the __________ of 6.294, so it is less.

6.13 is __________ than 6.294.

> **REMEMBER**
>
> As you move from left to right on a number line, the values increase.

6.13 ◯ 6.294

2   Use place value to compare.

1.380 ◯ 1.289

Step 1   Write each decimal, lining up the decimal points.

You can use a place-value chart if you wish.

1.380

1.289

> **THINK**
>
> The tenths and thousandths digits are both different, but the tenths place is greater than the thousandths place.

Step 2   Compare the decimals. Look for the greatest place where the digits are different.

The greatest place where the digits are different is the __________ place.

Step 3   Compare the digits.

3 is greater than 2, so 1.380 is __________ than 1.289.

1.380 ◯ 1.289

Independent Practice

1. When comparing two decimals, how do you know which digits to compare?

____

____

2. How could you use a number line to order three decimals from least to greatest?

____

____

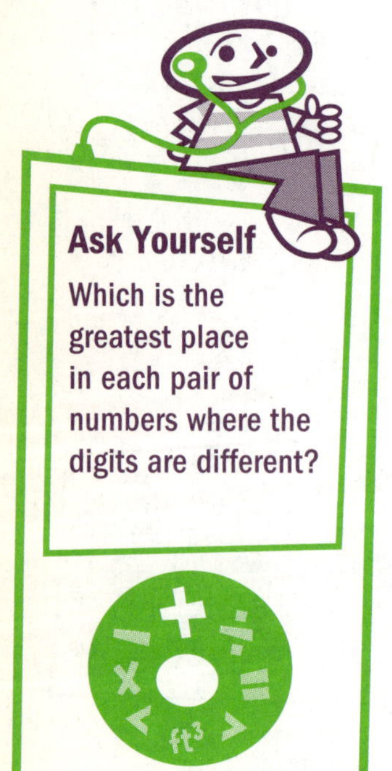

3. Use the place-value chart to compare 5.102 and 5.01. Write <, >, or =.

Ones	.	Tenths	Hundredths	Thousandths
	.			
	.			

5.102 ◯ 5.01

Compare. Write <, >, or =. You may wish to use a number line or a place-value chart.

4. 1.2 ◯ 1.5

5. 3.74 ◯ 3.70

6. 2.406 ◯ 2.415

7. 37.853 ◯ 37.853

8. Lisette is choosing between the tomato soup for $2.75 and the chicken soup for $2.69. Which soup is more expensive?

____

Compare. Write <, >, or =.

9. 0.45 ◯ 0.43

10. 0.209 ◯ 0.290

11. 6.80 ◯ 6.81

12. 15.296 ◯ 15.386

13. 24.002 ◯ 24.019

14. 476.812 ◯ 476.182

15. 3.95 ◯ 3.950

16. 79.069 ◯ 79.099

17. Which is less, 2.60 or 2.06? _________

18. Which is greater, 132.84 or 132.28? _________

Solve each problem.

19. At the Great Turtle Race, Mark's turtle crawled 2.85 meters. Janine's turtle crawled 2.98 meters. Which turtle crawled the greater distance?

____

20. At the turtle weigh-in, Mark's turtle is 11.82 ounces and Janine's turtle is 11.81 ounces. Which turtle weighs more?

____

21. At a 200-meter race, Zaid ran the distance in 34.5 seconds. Joey ran the race in 35.26 seconds, and Diego ran the race in 35.03 seconds. Who took the greatest amount of time to run the race?

____

Key Words

round

When you **round**, you are estimating the value of a number based on a given place value. To round a decimal, use the same rules as for rounding a whole number.

To round a decimal, look at the digit to the right of the place you are rounding to.

- If the digit is less than 5, round down.
- If the digit is 5 or greater, round up.

Example 1

Round 0.346 to the nearest hundredth.

Underline the place to which the number is being rounded.

0.3<u>4</u>6

Look at the digit to the right.

0.3<u>4</u>**6**

Since 6 is greater than 5, round the underlined digit up.
Drop all the digits to the right of the place you are rounding to.

To the nearest hundredth, 0.346 rounds to 0.35.

Example 2

Round 0.529 to the nearest tenth.

Use the rounding rules.

0.<u>5</u>29   Think: $2 < 5$

↓

0.5   Round down.

To the nearest tenth, 0.529 rounds to 0.5.

EXPLAIN

How would you round 6.854 to the nearest tenth?

Guided Practice

1 What is 9.037 rounded to the nearest tenth?

Step 1 Underline the place to which the
number is being rounded.

9.0̲37

Step 2 Look at the digit to the right.

9.0̲37

Step 3 Use the rounding rules.

9 . 0̲ 3 7   Think: $3 < 5$
↓   Round down.

9. ☐

9.037 rounded to the nearest tenth is __________.

2 What is 4.746 rounded to the nearest hundredth?

Step 1 Underline the place to which the
number is being rounded.

4.746

Step 2 Circle the digit to the right.

4.746

Step 3 Use the rounding rules.

4 . 7 4 6   Think: $6 > 5$
↓   Round up.

4 . 7 ☐

4.746 rounded to the nearest hundredth is __________.

Independent Practice

1. When rounding a decimal, how do you know whether to round up or down?

____

____

2. Explain why 7.498 rounded to the nearest tenth is 7.5.

____

____

Ask Yourself

What is the digit to the right of the place I am rounding to?

Is it less than, greater than, or equal to 5?

Round to the nearest tenth.

3. 0.16

4. 8.74

5. 1.628

_________   _________   _________

Round to the nearest hundredth.

6. 0.264

7. 0.539

8. 2.975

_________   _________   _________

Solve.

9. After hatching, a baby hummingbird has a mass of just 0.62 gram. What is its mass to the nearest tenth of a gram?

____

10. In one month, the town collected 1.348 tons of paper for recycling. What is the weight of the paper to the nearest hundredth of a ton?

____

Round 4.185 to the place named.

11. tenths

12. hundredths

13. ones

Round 0.273 to the place named.

14. tenths

15. hundredths

16. ones

Round each number to the place of the underlined digit.

17. 5.2̲5

18. 7.0̲6

19. 0.3̲14

20. 9.78̲2

21. 0.0̲39

22. 19̲.138

Solve each problem.

23. Taro bought a sports jersey for $17.95. To the nearest dollar, what did he pay?

24. A movie ticket costs $7.50. Elena tells Kesi the cost is about $8.00. Is $8.00 a reasonable estimate? Explain.

 Powers of Ten

Key Words

exponent

power

In the base-ten number system, **powers** of 10 are written as the number 10 with an **exponent**. An exponent shows how many times 10 is used as a factor.

$$10^3 \longleftarrow \text{exponent}$$

10^3 means $10 \times 10 \times 10$ or $1,000$

Look at the pattern in the table.

Base-Ten Numeral	Factors	Exponent Form
10	10	10^1
100	10×10	10^2
1000	$10 \times 10 \times 10$	10^3
10,000	$10 \times 10 \times 10 \times 10$	10^4
100,000	$10 \times 10 \times 10 \times 10 \times 10$	10^5

You can use the pattern in powers of 10 to mentally multiply whole numbers. To multiply a number by a power of 10, write zeros at the end of the number.

Example

Find the product of 18×10^4.

Use mental math. Decide how many zeros to place after the whole number.

$$18 \times 10^4 = 18 \times 10,000$$
$$= 18\mathbf{0,000} \longleftarrow \text{The exponent is 4, so write four zeros.}$$

DISCUSS

How can you use patterns of zeros to find the product of 40×10^3?

Guided Practice

1 What is the value of 10^6?

> **Step 1** Determine how many times 10 is used as a factor.
>
> In 10^6, the exponent is __________.
>
> 10 is used as a factor __________ times.
>
> **Step 2** Apply the pattern with powers of 10.
>
> The base-ten numeral for 10^6 has__________ zeros.

The value of 10^6 is ________________.

2 Find the product of 684×10^5.

> **Step 1** Decide how many zeros to place after 684.
>
> In 10^5, the exponent is __________.
>
> Write __________ zeros.
>
> **Step 2** Use mental math to multiply.
> Write the product.
>
> ________________________

$684 \times 10^5 =$ ________________

THINK

$684 \times 10^1 = 6,84\mathbf{0}$

$684 \times 10^2 = 68,4\mathbf{00}$

$684 \times 10^3 = 684,\mathbf{000}$

$684 \times 10^4 = 6,84\mathbf{0,000}$

REMEMBER

The exponent on a power of 10 is equal to the number of zeros in the product.

Independent Practice

1. How can you use mental math and what you know about powers of 10 to multiply 92,000 by 10^3?

   ____

   ____

2. A number has a 5 in the thousands place. You multiply the number by 10. Where will the 5 be in the product? Explain.

   ____

   ____

3. Complete the table to show the pattern in multiplying powers of 10.

Factors	Factors in Exponent Form	Product
9×10	9×10^1	90
$9 \times 10 \times 10$	9×10^2	900

Use mental math to find the product.

4. $35 \times 100 =$ __________

5. $29 \times 10^4 =$ __________

6. $6,900 \times 100 =$ __________

7. $15,000 \times 10^3 =$ __________

8. At a garden shop, one tree costs $100. A school buys 24 trees to plant around its playground. What is the total cost of the trees?

   ____

Multiply.

9. 72×100

10. $5 \times 1{,}000$

11. $60 \times 1{,}000$

12. $1{,}800 \times 100$

13. 359×1000

14. $20{,}000 \times 100$

15. 52×10^2

16. 149×10^3

17. 9×10^7

18. 900×10^2

19. 410×10^4

20. $7{,}300 \times 10^3$

Solve each problem.

21. Cristin runs 10 miles each day in her preparations to run the marathon. How many miles will she run in 31 days?

22. Paper is sold in boxes of 1,000 sheets each. The Byrd Company orders 50 boxes. How many sheets of paper is this?

23. What is the rule for the number pattern?

25; 250; 2,500; 25,000; 250,000

When multiplying a decimal by a power of 10, use the exponent to decide how many places to move the decimal point to the right.

When dividing a decimal by a power of 10, use the exponent to decide how many places to move the decimal point to the left.

Example 1

Find the product of 7.53×10^3.

Decide how many places to move the decimal point to the right.

$7.53 \times 10^1 = 75.3$ ⟵ Move the decimal point one place to the right.

$7.53 \times 10^2 = 753$ ⟵ Move the decimal point two places to the right.

$7.53 \times 10^3 = 7,530$ ⟵ Move the decimal point three place to the right.

$7.53 \times 10^3 = 7,530$

Example 2

Find the quotient of $3.9 \div 10^2$.

Decide how many places to move the decimal point to the left.

$3.9 \div 10^1 = 0.39$ ⟵ Move the decimal point one place to the left.

$3.9 \div 10^2 = 0.039$ ⟵ Move the decimal point two places to the left.

$3.9 \div 10^2 = 0.039$

DISCUSS

When multiplying or dividing a decimal by a power of 10, how do you decide how many places to move the decimal point?

Guided Practice

1 Find the product of 0.849×10^4.

    Step 1 Decide how many places to move the decimal point to the right.

    In 10^4, the exponent is __________.

    Move the decimal point __________ places to the right.

    Step 2 Write the product.

    ____

    $0.849 \times 10^4 =$ __________

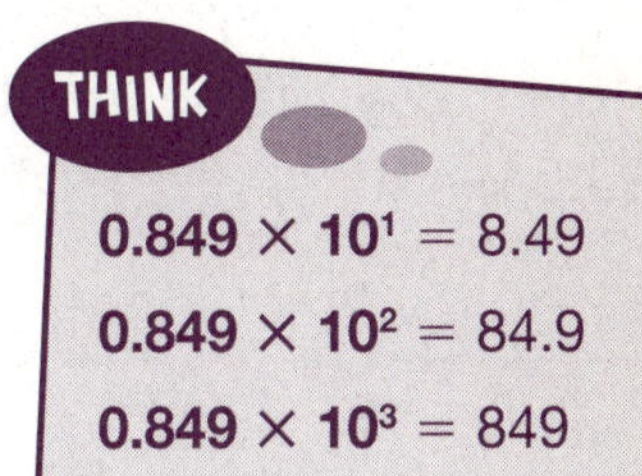

2 Find the quotient of $12.5 \div 10^3$.

    Step 1 Decide how many places to move the decimal point to the left.

    In 10^3, the exponent is __________.

    Move the decimal point __________ places to the left.

    Step 2 Write the quotient.

    ____

    $12.5 \div 10^3 =$ __________

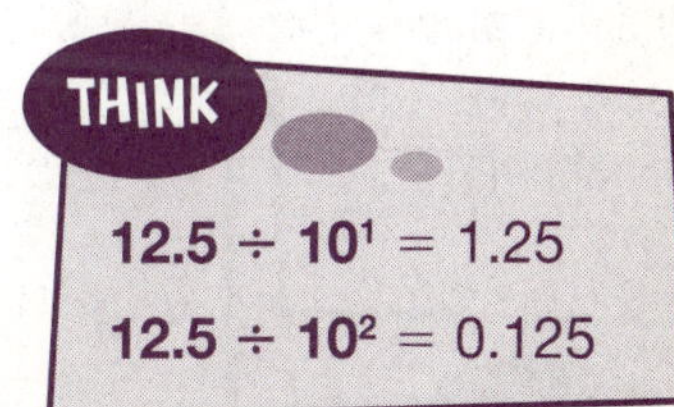

Independent Practice

1. How can you use mental math and what you know about powers of 10 to multiply 58.7 by 10^3?

____

____

2. How can you use mental math and what you know about powers of 10 to divide 93.5 by 10^2?

____

____

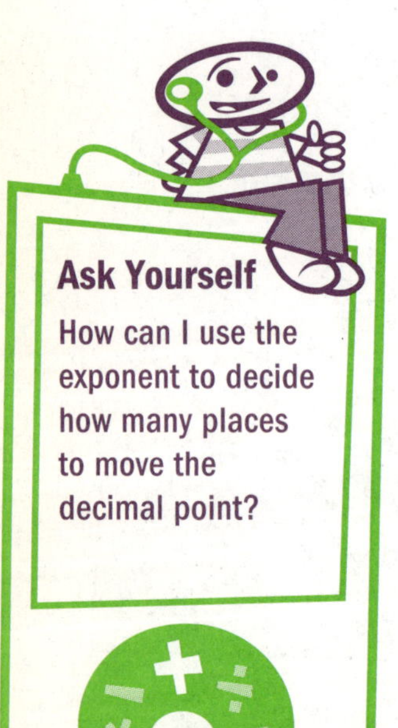

Ask Yourself

How can I use the exponent to decide how many places to move the decimal point?

Use mental math to find the product or quotient.

3. $6.1 \times 10^2 =$ __________

4. $35.2 \times 10^4 =$ __________

5. $4.79 \times 10 =$ __________

6. $8.09 \times 10^2 =$ __________

7. $9.7 \div 10^1 =$ __________

8. $18.4 \div 10^2 =$ __________

9. $100.7 \div 10^3 =$ __________

10. $27.61 \div 10^2 =$ __________

11. During a fund-raiser, Angie sold 100 pots of tulips for $4.95 each. How much did she earn? Hint: $100 = 10^2$

____

12. Ismael sold 10 packets of seeds. If he raised $25.00, what is the cost of one packet of seeds? Hint: $10 = 10^1$

____

Multiply.

13. 1.25×10^2

14. 4.0×10^3

15. 67.8×10^3

____

____

____

16. 0.37×10^4

17. 4.19×10^5

18. 0.015×10^5

____

____

____

Divide.

19. $47.14 \div 10^2$

20. $5.96 \div 10^1$

21. $216.7 \div 10^3$

____

____

____

22. $328.4 \div 10^2$

23. $7,159.32 \div 10^4$

24. $5,836.01 \div 10^3$

____

____

____

Solve each problem.

Use the prices in the table.

25. During the football season, Joe sold 1,000 hamburgers. How much money did he earn selling hamburgers?

____

26. During half-time, Joe sold $175.00 worth of hot dogs. How many hot dogs was that?

____

Joe's Place	
Hamburgers	$2.90
Hot dogs	$1.75
Fries	$2.00

When you **add** two numbers, the answer is the **sum**.
You add decimals in the same way you add whole numbers.
Just remember to line up the decimal points, then place the
decimal point in the sum.

Example

In September, 1.86 inches of rain fell. In October, 0.57 inches of rain fell.
What is the total rainfall for the two months?

Find the sum of 1.86 and 0.57.

Write the problem vertically.
Line up the decimal points to align place-value positions.

$$\begin{array}{r} 1.86 \\ +\ 0.57 \\ \hline \end{array}$$

Add the hundredths. Regroup if you need to.

$$\begin{array}{r} 1 \\ 1.8\mathbf{6} \\ +\ 0.5\mathbf{7} \\ \hline \mathbf{3} \end{array}$$

Add the tenths. Regroup if you need to.

$$\begin{array}{r} 1\ \mathbf{1} \\ 1.\mathbf{8}6 \\ +\ 0.\mathbf{5}7 \\ \hline \mathbf{4}3 \end{array}$$

Add the ones. Place the
decimal point in the sum.

$$\begin{array}{r} \mathbf{1}\ 1 \\ \mathbf{1}.86 \\ +\ \mathbf{0}.57 \\ \hline \mathbf{2}.43 \end{array}$$

The total rainfall for the two months is
2.43 inches.

ANALYZE

When adding decimals, why is it
important to write the decimal point
in the correct place in the sum?

Guided Practice

Find the sum.

2.62 + 3.7

Step 1   Write the problem vertically.
Line up the decimal points to
align place-value positions.

```
  2.62
+ 3.70   ⟵── Place a zero for an
                equivalent decimal.
```

THINK

3.7 = 3.70
3.7 and 3.70 are
equivalent decimals.

Step 2   Add the hundredths. Regroup if needed.

```
  2.62
+ 3.70
     2
```

Step 3   Add the tenths. Regroup if needed.

THINK

6 + 7 = 13
Write a 3 in the tenths place
and regroup the 10 tenths
as 1 one.

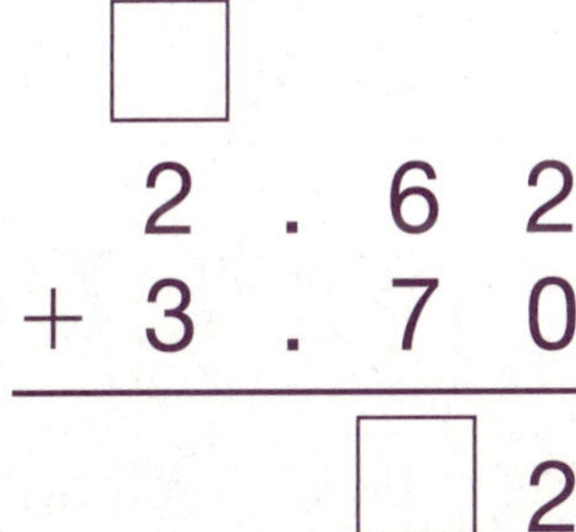

```
    □
  2 . 6 2
+ 3 . 7 0
    □   2
```

Step 4   Add the ones. Place the decimal point in the sum.

```
    □
  2 . 6 2
+ 3 . 7 0
  □   □ 2
```

2.62 + 3.7 = __________

Independent Practice

1. Explain how to find the sum of two decimals.

____

____

2. When adding decimals, when is it helpful to show an equivalent decimal?

____

____

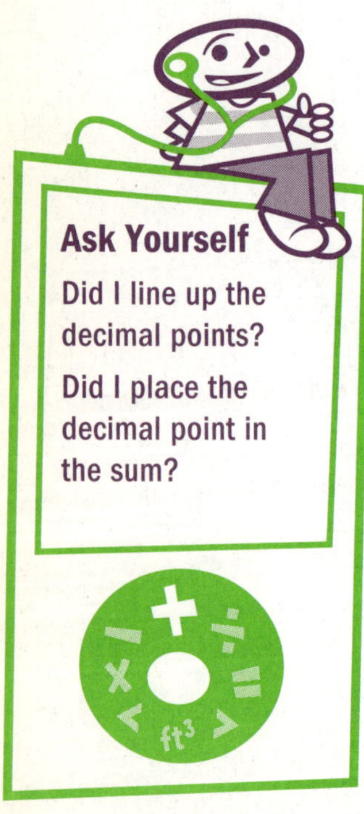

For questions 3 through 6, write the problem vertically. Then find the sum.

3. $0.9 + 0.8$

4. $1.37 + 2.34$

5. $1.48 + 0.53$

6. $4.69 + 3.21$

7. In January, 2.3 inches of snow fell. In February, 6.8 inches fell. What was the total snowfall for the two months?

____

8. Cheri has \$4.82. She receives \$5.50 for walking a dog. How much money does she have now?

____

Find each sum.

9. 5.7 + 6.8

10. 4.24 + 1.85

11. 5.07 + 0.38

12. 9.45 + 0.7

13. 18.31 + 10.06

14. 32.9 + 8.54

15. 0.18 + 1.93

16. 7.7 + 0.12

17. 8.65 + 6.91

18. 20.1 + 0.35

19. 16.7 + 0.83

20. 10.9 + 0.04

Solve each problem.

21. The rainfall for three months is: May—3.2 inches, June—1.78 inches, and July—2.06 inches. What is the total rainfall for the three months?

____

22. Rob ordered dinner at a restaurant for $21.99. The tax on his dinner is $1.32. How much does Rob owe?

____

14 Subtract Decimals

When you **subtract** two numbers, the answer is the **difference**. You subtract decimals in the same way you subtract whole numbers. Just remember to line up the decimal points, then place the decimal point in the difference.

Example

In one week, a pea plant grew from 3.46 centimeters to 5.27 centimeters. How many centimeters did the pea plant grow in one week?

Find the difference of 3.46 and 5.27.

Write the problem vertically.
Line up the decimal points to align place-value positions.

```
  5.27
− 3.46
```

Subtract the hundredths.

```
  5.27
− 3.46
     1
```

Subtract the tenths, regrouping as necessary.

```
  4 12
  5.27
− 3.46
    81
```

Subtract the ones. Place the decimal point in the difference.

```
  4 12
  5.27
− 3.46
  1.81
```

The pea plant grew 1.81 centimeters.

APPLY

How would you align 5.36 − 4.1 when writing the problem vertically?

Guided Practice

Find the difference.

8.5 − 4.63

Step 1 Write the problem vertically.
Line up the decimal points.

8.5**0** ⟵— Place a zero for an
− 4.63   equivalent decimal.

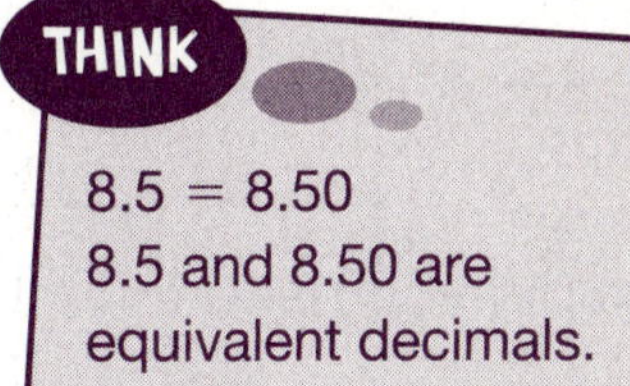

Step 2 Subtract the hundredths. Regroup if needed.

```
    4 10
 8.5̶0̶
− 4.63
─────
     7
```

Step 3 Subtract the tenths. Regroup if needed.

```
 □      14  10
 8̶ . 5̶  0̶
− 4 . 6  3
─────────
        □ 7
```


Step 4 Subtract the ones. Place the decimal point in the difference.

```
 □      14  10
 8̶ . 5̶  0̶
− 4 . 6  3
─────────
 □    □ 7
```

8.5 − 4.63 = __________

Independent Practice

1. Explain how to find the difference of two decimals.

____

____

2. Why did you need to write an equivalent decimal when subtracting $8.5 - 4.63$?

____

____

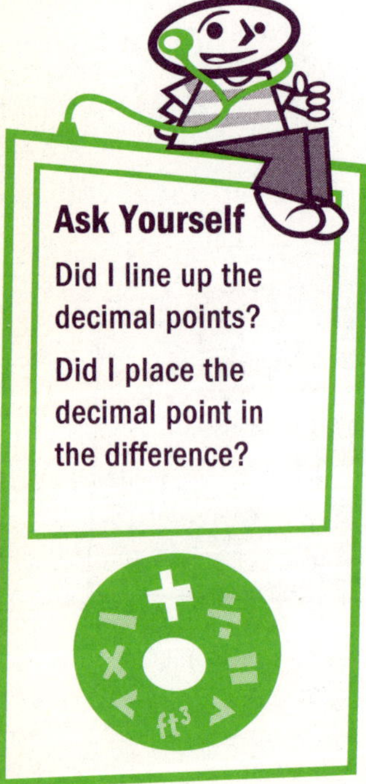

Ask Yourself

Did I line up the decimal points?

Did I place the decimal point in the difference?

For questions 3 through 6, write the problem vertically. Then find the difference.

3. $0.7 - 0.5$

4. $4.27 - 2.14$

5. $3.89 - 0.89$

6. $9.45 - 6.17$

7. The regular price of a video game is $23.97. During a sale, the price is $19.95. How much will you save by buying the game on sale?

____

8. Dwayne is buying a video game for $17.57. He gives the clerk a $20 bill. How much change will he receive?

____

Find each difference.

9. $6.4 - 3.8$

10. $5.2 - 2.9$

11. $4.18 - 0.24$

12. $0.86 - 0.77$

13. $4.37 - 2.5$

14. $13.76 - 8.5$

15. $6.3 - 1.47$

16. $8.02 - 4.73$

17. $1.5 - 0.81$

18. $4.61 - 1.34$

19. $10.82 - 3.95$

20. $3.6 - 1.09$

Solve each problem.

21. Mr. Ruiz fills up his gas tank with 56.2 liters of gasoline. After driving for an hour, the tank has 48 liters of gasoline left. How much gasoline did his car use?

____

22. Emma earned $15.00 babysitting. She bought a book for $8.99 and a snack for $2.50. How much money does she have left?

____

When you multiply decimals, you do not need to line up the decimal points. First, multiply the decimals the same way you multiply whole numbers. Then use estimation or count decimal places in the factors to place the decimal point in the product.

Example

Find the product of 6.2 and 0.7.

Estimate the product. Round each factor.
6.2 rounds to 6. 0.7 rounds to 1.
$6 \times 1 = 6$
The product is about 6.

Write the problem vertically. Multiply as with whole numbers.

$$\begin{array}{r} 1 \\ 6.2 \\ \times\ 0.7 \\ \hline 434 \end{array}$$

Use the estimate to place the decimal point in the product.

$$\begin{array}{r} 6.2 \\ \times\ 0.7 \\ \hline 4.34 \end{array}$$

⟵ Since the estimate is 6, place the decimal point so there is a one-digit whole number in the product.

Or, you can count decimal places in the factors to place the decimal point in the product.

$$\begin{array}{r} 6.2 \\ \times\ 0.7 \\ \hline 4.34 \end{array}$$

6.2 ⟵ 1 decimal place
× 0.7 ⟵ 1 decimal place
4.34 ⟵ 2 decimal places in the product

$6.2 \times 0.7 = 4.34$

GENERALIZE

How many decimal places are in the product of 2.8×0.04? Explain your reasoning.

Guided Practice

Find the product.

2.93 × 1.5

Step 1 Estimate the product.

2.93 rounds to _________.

1.5 rounds to _________.

_________ × _________ = _________

Step 2 Write the problem vertically.
Then multiply as with whole numbers.
Regroup as needed.

$$\begin{array}{r} 2.93 \\ \times\ \ 1.5 \\ \hline 1465 \\ +\ 2930 \end{array}$$

REMEMBER
You do not need to line up the decimal points.

Step 3 Find the total number of decimal places
in the factors. Place the decimal point
that number of places from the right in the product.

$$\begin{array}{r} 2.9\ 3 \\ \times\ \ \ \ \ \ 1.5 \\ \hline 1\ 4\ 6\ 5 \\ +\ 2\ 9\ 3\ 0 \end{array}$$

2.9 3 ← 2 decimal places

1.5 ← 1 decimal place

□□□□ ← □ decimal places

THINK
The total number of decimal places in the factors equals the number of decimal places in the product.

2.93 × 1.5 = _____________

Independent Practice

1. How can you use estimation to check that your product is reasonable?

2. How do you multiply two decimal numbers?

Ask Yourself

Does the product have the correct number of decimal places?

Did I use estimation to check that my answer is reasonable?

Write how many decimal places each product will have.

3. 8×2.67

_______ place(s)

4. 0.3×14

_______ place(s)

5. 1.2×0.57

_______ place(s)

Estimate the product. Then find the exact answer.

6. 5×3.9

Estimate: _______

Exact: _______

7. 1.8×24

Estimate: _______

Exact: _______

8. 13×0.62

Estimate: _______

Exact: _______

9. 1.25×3

Estimate: _______

Exact: _______

10. Mr. Gomez's class is taking a trip to an aquarium. Tickets cost $14.95. If Mr. Gomez buys 29 tickets, how much will it cost?

____

Find the product. Estimate to check.

11. 0.2 × 15

12. 3.9 × 0.8

13. 5.6 × 24

14. 12 × 0.03

15. 0.5 × 0.5

16. 8.6 × 0.1

17. 0.62 × 0.4

18. 1.37 × 0.6

19. 11.73 × 0.9

20. 7.3 × 0.02

21. 3.85 × 19

22. 0.51 × 0.7

Solve each problem.

23. For an experiment, Sharonda has 3 beakers.
She puts 1.75 mL of acetic acid into each beaker.
How many milliliters of acetic acid did she use?

____

24. For the school picnic, Ms. Wright buys 15 packages
of hot dog buns for $1.29 each. What is the total cost
of the buns?

____

To divide a decimal by a whole number, first place the decimal point in the quotient above the decimal point in the dividend. Then divide as with whole numbers. Finally, check by multiplying.

Example

Find the quotient of 4.95 and 3.

Write the decimal point of the quotient above the decimal point of the dividend.

$$3 \overline{)4.95}$$

Divide as with whole numbers.

```
     1.65
3 ) 4.95
   -3        ← 1 × 3 = 3
    1 9
   -1 8      ← 6 × 3 = 18
      15
    - 15     ← 5 × 3 = 15
       0
```

Multiply to check your quotient.

```
   1.65
 ×    3
   4.95
```

The product equals the dividend. The quotient is correct.

$$4.95 \div 3 = 1.65$$

COMPARE

How is dividing a decimal by a whole number like dividing a whole number by a whole number? How is it different?

Guided Practice

Find the quotient.

5.04 ÷ 8

Step 1   Write the decimal point of the quotient above
the decimal point of the dividend.

$$8\overline{)5.04}$$

Step 2   Divide as you would divide whole numbers.

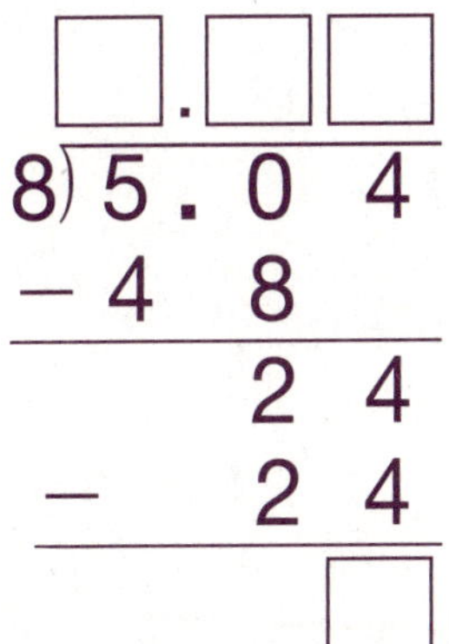

```
  □.□□
8)5.0 4
 -4 8
    2 4
 -    2 4
       □
```

THINK

The divisor is greater
than the ones in the
dividend, so place a
0 in the ones place of
the quotient.

Step 3   Check the answer.
Multiply the quotient by the divisor.

□.□□   ← quotient

×   □   ← divisor

□.□□   ← This equals the dividend. The quotient is correct.

5.04 ÷ 8 = _______

Independent Practice

1. Explain where to place the decimal point in the quotient when dividing a decimal by a whole number.

____

____

2. How can you check your quotient when you divide a decimal by a whole number?

____

____

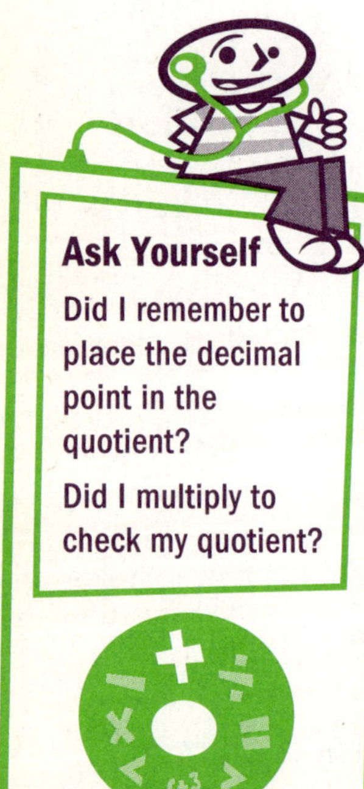

Ask Yourself

Did I remember to place the decimal point in the quotient?

Did I multiply to check my quotient?

Place the decimal point in the quotient.

3.　$\quad 3\ 2$
$4\overline{)1\ 2.8}$

4.　$\quad 1\ 5\ 4$
$6\overline{)9.2\ 4}$

5.　$\quad 0\ 8\ 6$
$2\overline{)1.7\ 2}$

Divide. Check by multiplying.

6. $7\overline{)1.4}$

7. $3\overline{)13.5}$

8. $8\overline{)4.8}$

9. $5\overline{)7.0}$

10. Gina walks 4.8 miles in 2 hours. How far does she walk in 1 hour?

____

Find the quotient. Check your answer.

11. $7\overline{)4.9}$ **12.** $5\overline{)0.45}$ **13.** $2\overline{)1.06}$ **14.** $3\overline{)13.8}$

15. $10\overline{)25.10}$ **16.** $16\overline{)36.8}$ **17.** $8\overline{)43.2}$ **18.** $9\overline{)10.35}$

19. $6.75 \div 3$ **20.** $14.60 \div 4$ **21.** $45.12 \div 6$

22. $1.56 \div 4$ **23.** $60.8 \div 32$ **24.** $0.84 \div 14$

Solve each problem.

25. A dozen eggs costs $2.88. What is the cost of 1 egg?

____

26. Four cans of soup cost $6.76. What is the cost of 1 can of soup?

____

add a mathematical operation that results in a sum (Page 52)

coordinate plane a grid formed by a horizontal line called the *x*-axis and a vertical line called the *y*-axis (Page 16)

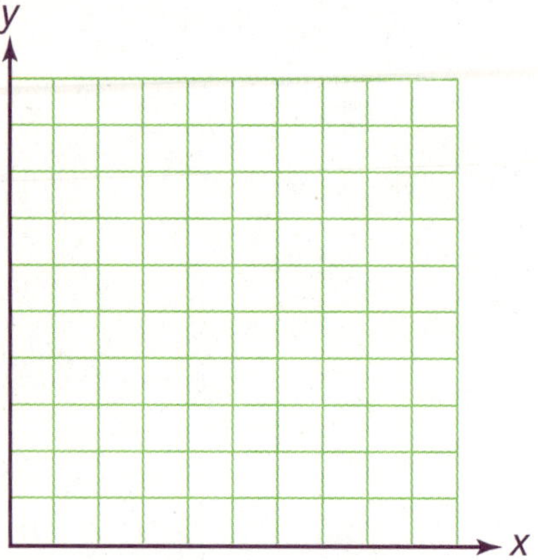

decimal a number that names wholes and parts of a whole (Page 32)

Example: 2.59

decimal point in a decimal number, separates the ones from the tenths (Page 32)

difference the answer to a subtraction problem (Page 56)

divide a mathematical operation that results in a quotient (Page 24)

dividend the number being divided (Page 24)

divisor the number by which you divide (Page 24)

equation a statement that two expressions are equal (Page 28)

Example: $4 + 3 = 5 + 2$

exponent a number that tells how many times a number is used as a factor (Page 44)

Example: 7^3 The exponent is 3.

expression a combination of numbers and operations (Page 4)

multiply a mathematical operation that results in a product (Page 20)

number pattern a list of numbers that follow a certain order (Page 12)

number sequence a list of numbers (Page 12)

operation signs mathematical signs such as $+$, $-$, $\times$, and $\div$ (Page 4)

ordered pair a pair of numbers (x, y) that shows a point on a coordinate grid (Page 16)

order of operations a set of rules for solving an expression with more than one operation (Page 8)

parentheses symbols ( ) that show which operation to do first (Page 4)

power the number of times a number is used as a factor (Page 44)

product the answer to a multiplication problem (Page 20)

quotient the answer to a division problem (Page 24)

remainder the amount left over when a number cannot be divided equally (Page 24)

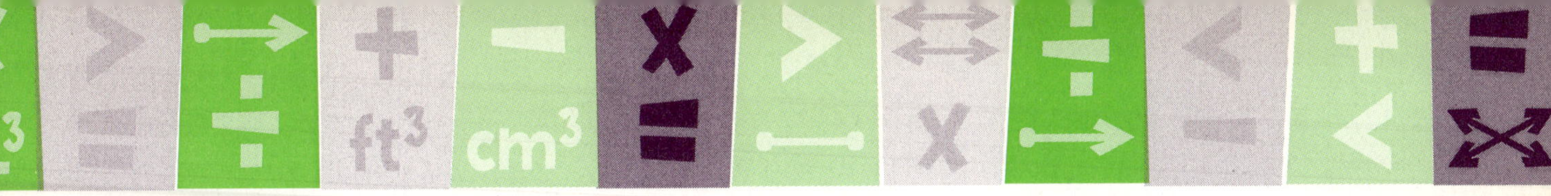

round to increase or decrease to the nearest place value (Page 40)

rule a way to describe a number sequence or pattern (Page 12)

subtract a mathematical operation that results in a difference (Page 56)

sum the answer to an addition problem (Page 52)

term a number or figure in a pattern or expression (Page 12)

x*-coordinate** first number in an ordered pair (x***, *y*) (Page 16)

y*-coordinate** second number in an ordered pair (*x*, ***y) (Page 16)

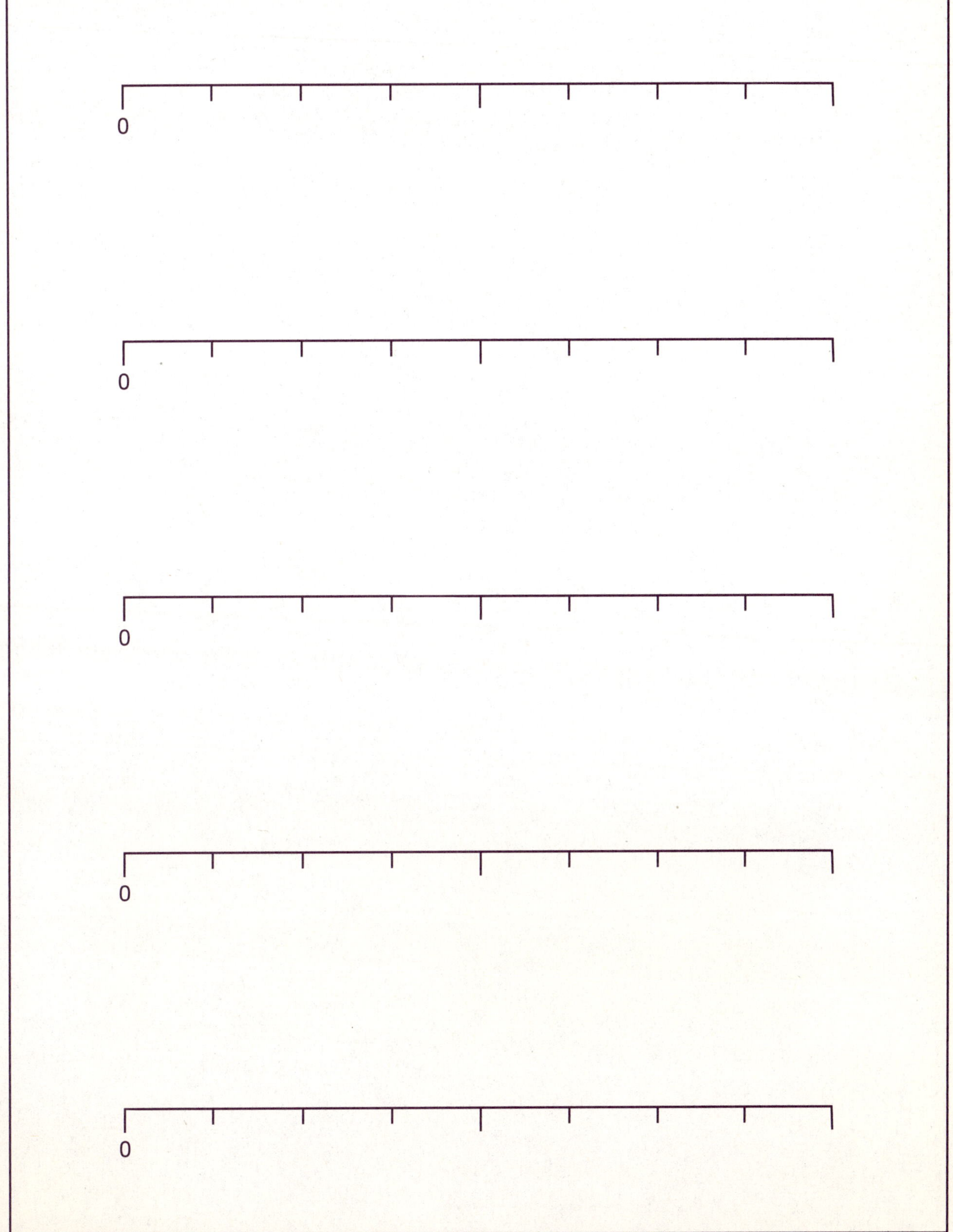

0
0
0
0
0

Math Tools: Decimal Place-Value Charts

Hundreds	Tens	Ones	.	Tenths	Hundredths	Thousandths

Hundreds	Tens	Ones	.	Tenths	Hundredths	Thousandths

Hundreds	Tens	Ones	.	Tenths	Hundredths	Thousandths

Hundreds	Tens	Ones	.	Tenths	Hundredths	Thousandths

Notes

Notes

Notes